The Broken Fall

A Katrina Collection

TONI ORRILL

HAMILTON BOOKS

A member of

THE ROWMAN & LITTLEFIELD PUBLISHING GROUP

Lanham • Boulder • New York • Toronto • Plymouth, UK

Hamilton Books
4501 Forbes Boulevard
Suite 200
Lanham, Maryland 20706
Hamilton Books Acquisitions Department (301) 459-3366

Estover Road
Plymouth PL6 7PY
United Kingdom

Library of Congress Control Number: 2009925331
ISBN: 978-0-7618-4540-9 (paperback : alk. paper)
eISBN: 978-0-7618-4541-6

∞™ The paper used in this publication meets the minimum
requirements of American National Standard for Information
Sciences—Permanence of Paper for Printed Library Materials,
ANSI Z39.48—1984

For A.D. Jenkins and Lester Muller—
Both great Southern gentlemen

Contents

CONTENTS

Acknowledgments

In Appreciation of Those Who Supported this Work—
The Editorial Board of
Rowman & Littlefield Publishing Group
Brooke Bascietto and Patti Belcher of Hamilton Books
Susan Davis *for her editing*
Elise and Sissy *for reviewing the manuscript*
Margaret O'Connell *for her hospitality*
The towns of Covington, Lafayette and Natchitoches in
Louisiana; and Subiaco, Arkansas—
All for hosting me along this journey

Introduction

I have always led an orderly life—or shall I say—life has always ordered my journey, carving its path through my heart like a stubborn river bent on hearing its own roar. Eventually, one chooses only freedom or security, for in their valley, is simply existence.

This I know for certain.

Though most understanding keeps a mystery, or shall I say that the answers we seek may never strike at midnight, my soul, once small and cautious of its own stand, was uncovered and grown from an unspeakable rain that blossomed wisdom from the dunes of soundless pain.

The fall began with a black twist of luck, swirling into a whirlpool of absent nights and unfortunate days. Her name I dare not mention for she is very well cursed, a scarlet scar best forgotten than explained. You, reader, must only know that when she, our unfriendly master, arrived, we, her study of resilience, obeyed.

I admit she is to blame for the pages of inspiration in your hands. I nod to her influence, for no matter how desperate and scornful, her mark gave way to a rebirth of spirit and rallies of passion.

For through her vicious teaching, one learned to embrace the dark, then sift its fine color with grace; to empty everything spelled from the soul, and restore it with the love of God who knows you wherever you are, even in the sage of the wild.

Imagine fastening sense to nothingness, life calmed only by fear. And after her grisly circular shadow stormed our night, morning landed like the starling in a bottomless world of abundance.

This work holds no more than your own belief, illuminated only by your candle in the corner of solitude. Remember her, you may, for you are indeed holder of her flame, watcher of the progress of an unforgettable people forever unchanged.

Her name was Katrina.

Toni Orrill
August, 2007

ONE

Ravine

Times are hard, and change has toppled the mossy landscape by the roots, ravaging all greens to the frown of brown. A mixture of raw frustration and fatigue clenches the will, where a dark hole of silt has been deposited, fields of rice swamped before harvest.

In this ravine, mail forgets its own address, mothers are teachers, fathers jobless, and living quarters unlivable. Hope dissolves like the baby marsh grass, smoothed by the abrasive ripples pretending to be the gentle stroke of nature's hand.

Our heads try to stave off the waves of despair that find no sanctuary from the water's needs. When did man take charge of His land, toiling and soiling with hands of greed, a boot walked into loyal holes, the patina of cypress reflecting alone?

With each day comes the strange expectation to remain active in a modern world, the only tools of life a rake and broom. Our possessions are greater—candles, bleach, soap, and a brush; bibles, books and photographs now buried beneath the fishermen's village.

Unfairness is as even as where engraved hills touch the floating south, the lake a drink of southern comfort for heirlooms of oysters and parks of deer. There, organdy swaggers skiffs, the wind whistles Dixie and the water sings the blues.

I am a patriot, modern and natural, discovering faith in the city before moving in God's direction to the land I now sow. A heart moored in the south, a soul sailed to the north.

I know, like myself, God has no favorites, nor has He shown wrath to either side. Instead, we inhabitants have stirred our own creation, now taste and see only mercy.

He is our only protection through this periscope of hope.

TWO

Harbor

Home is where God is, and explains the very ground we stand on—where memories of childhood sleep on feathers of peace, and hearts take root like the profusion of violets on the sill in spring.

The kind of land you lived on forges a signet on the soul; for myself, it was a place of pomegranates and honey walls, a pine-lined cottage where a still pond broke the gravel road.

On weekends our family passed, like quail on a prayer, to the sandbanks of this harbor, delighting when the gulf sun bent bark into animal faces and moonlight made puppets on clouds of sheets. I am certain now the eyes of the Lord were always upon the sweeping knotted porch, finding us dreaming in tiny beds as many as the number of sheep.

Days were long and happy in that small town, or perhaps the smiles just make it look easier, simpler like the penny-store, where seafood needed only a pot of boiling water and a heart of gold to stir friendship.

There, like here, we came to understand life and know contentment, our follies listening for train whistles and paddling against the foamy waves, nodding at neighbors, and learning humility at the stamp-size post office at the bend.

Papa was Irish host on weekends and town mayor on holidays. He would jig and sing on occasions of happiness, simmering up the stove for dinner well before breakfast.

We learned to swim against the briny current to busts of love, and float on schools of perch to the deep side of the shoals. Visiting cooled the afternoon, cards dealt with the evening swarms of see-ums.

There, a pledge was a promise, a man's word just his proper name. Ours was baptized and blessed in love and honor, proudly hung like the cross at the doorstep, a precious hat too fine to keep in the bureau.

We knew the thing that good was, a land of water that still whiffs sentiment, its salty perfume faithfully held in a trust of ivory, until uncorked at my bedside.

Tonight, the linens breathe its luscious scent while above my heart rests a bear on watch, his buttery eyes etched between the beams, nappy coat tucked into the night ahead.

To this creature of comfort, I cry when the day hurts and family is afar. Under his care, I recall love surviving storms and I am again just a girl of God.

THREE

Indigo

Our hearts are full of compassion, and I am learning to grieve for another while embittered by the same blow, like the good widow offering condolences to her man's best friend, preaching and praising when it is best to believe, to embrace the idea that the South will revolve with new days again, care certain to drift downstream to our melancholy docks.

I am loving our neighbors of America, growing together through the thrashing like hayseeds, finding through their gentle acts of graciousness, that the most common of people share the common purpose of humanity.

How brightly and softly we stand when crocheted into this quilt of goodwill, spreading indigo stripes and night stars along welcome maps, entertaining lost angels unaware.

Its blue is the hope of light, as necessary to the prism as the food and water our hunger learned to ration, a deep purple so radiant that all hues of beings depend upon its brilliance to draw their values into a smile of dignity.

From these depths of autumn, we pilgrims see rainbows of hands through the blackened sky, humbled now to find daily bread in the kindness of strangers, charity in rooms of a nation echoing with grace.

All happily equal are we now as the power of love balances on a delta of peace, our heritage under God finally fitting the spirit, speaking louder than words of freedom and faith.

For His love is one for all, and I stand patiently with an amazed heart of pride.

FOUR

Lullaby

As day closes its weary lid, I honor time as never before in these deep lovely hours, beholding the light of eyes flashing peacefully as they reach paradise. The homeward journey has polished these jewels into the soft aquamarines of sailors, beaten an old heart into the solid rubies of pirates.

There was no spiritual compass to magnetize their bearing, just the sheer will to set a sweetheart free from the shipwreck on a coast of everglades and birds of many colors. I marvel at his mapped hands, calloused by love, a gripping valentine sealed in a tanned bottle. They rest on his panting chest like a fallen steeple in a stiff room of a sweet bay, pinned to tight ropes on a post of modern science.

For precisely four nights and three days, his sugared voice no longer spread its infectious joy, but his giving still overflows as a rush of honesty on a barren bank.

In this hardest, coldest cave of rest, I finally met my father, became daughter to a man, knew the emotion of the beloved, or in this case, was given another, grandfather, a man of God who loved me as his own.

For all the searching, the holes of wondering and believing, I was just a star without a suitable constellation, I am now a Venus born to an amazing sun.

His gravity was there all along, radiating pride and warmth, grounding my restive search of the sky for direction, a birthname in the glittering vista.

How it would be easy to jump onto his ship, stay in the nostalgic cusp of departure, but heavenly life is not ready for my visit, myself ill-prepared to find peaceful perfection.

I am still in great transition, a work unfinished, a glowing spirit bound by natural force to seek its own path before discovering a supernatural other.

Let go, I pray, your Master is waiting and I wave our lullaby goodbye.

FIVE

Evensong

A dappled friend arrived unannounced, terribly tardy for lunch, yet especially early for dinner, certain of this address on the screen. He began pushing and pecking my way, like the hungry diner bossily cutting the crowd in two, special in his own mind, unable to stand another second without satisfaction.

He could not wait either to break the illusion of his presence, scratchy claws grasping the fine grey shield, cold liquid eyes staring like beads of a feathered mask, begging for just a glance.

Sensing all instincts, I leap high as a dormer thrown at the sight of hope, a drying land. Had a visitor not been a luxury nor the haziness of the clouds exhausted the afternoon, the idea to receive this fellow would have simply been an afterthought, a walk-by or drive-along on my tunneled path, but on this particular day, with no real tidings to acknowledge, I commission him as bearer of good news, and imagine his very knock a branch of change.

If you have made it through, our God caring enough for you, tell of your pain, for certainly the sky sees our plight, and hears your cry, a bittersweet arrival like the homecoming of a soldier still torn by war. All are happy with the return but still too clearly recall the nature of farewell.

Now, I hear his evensong brightening the grim dusk and remember all of the sparrows alone on the housetops I watched, seemingly abandoned yet promised provision, and how forgotten they felt before the whirling birds swooped them off to shelter.

Again and again, he adamantly knocks, pressing for something he knows beyond the window we see. What has he lost I wonder? And when will he accept it is no longer there?

We spend this year as a tale that was foretold, waiting on a word, clutching the lesson we must all re-learn as we rebuild—this is it here, and our reflections can only be the face of God. Nothing else is left. No one else is home in this broken house of glass.

SIX

Driftwood

Last night I filled my lamp with oil wondering at what hour love would cautiously turn the door handle—myself upside down with desire, him usually unsure if it would be right, too late or too telling. A cross wind on the longest bridge, he brings inconvenient excitement, and I find myself opening the windows after dark, expecting his musky breeze to arouse the air.

If He knows my thoughts, looks at my heart, why do I long to feel the beat of this driftwood cross, lonely yet wary of this refuge, a place of love unconditionally frightening and most comfortable on the occasion of tonight?

I detect reservation in the slow crawl of my coral-collared prize, prideful legs clung to the floor like a figurine, confused eyes rigid in the clear midnight rain.

How does love step forward just once, then, draw into reverse, creep into the heart in such a way to make each step count, then stop perfectly short before disappearing into night?

Which is it, I wonder, come or go, or show you care but not so much to stay?

If a lizard can be caught in the hand, he is almost worthy of fondness, even if in this particular palace my persuasion is only an outstretched neck, plain and long, refusing to run and chase, compromise, or lace his shoes to our souls.

If our Father can be seen in even the most hardened of hearts, I feel His love in the most restless of men. If Jesus forgave the impure, I love the uncommitted and unsure. Jesus prayed forgive them, I whisper mercy when they sin, stumble and leave.

He has made known to him my name, and love is here if he stays more than tonight.

SEVEN

Phoenix

The world is crashing, sky passing us by, despite the signs we flail into the heady vapor of aftermath. At the kissing point, where destiny and the divine distance themselves, discomfort has made landfall on the wings of the phoenix, chaos ablaze in the sweltering masquerade of civility.

To remain human in the savage is a grand expectation, a deed as elusive as a whale finding shore or any other place where life cannot breathe easily.

How do miracles arise from such misery?

Our plight is a spectacle of the unusual, a freak of survival, and one cannot help but feel like the last born arriving long after the others have opened their eyes to the world.

Behind. Out of touch.

We are a step farther out, I fear, than intended, plucked from our twigged huts so quickly into a stirring moral storm so fierce, one can only understand the lashing of nature's leash by being tied to the landscape of its luminous floor.

When a soul flusters with this type of shakedown, it is all but too ambitious not to look down while falling into the frightening crimson, and confident white waves, to not long for the love of a nest, small, broken or simply ravaged.

To be lost is to feel erased, unknown until further notice, stolen by force without a shrill for ransom. And there, only there, can one truly appreciate what it means to be reborn, to glide mystically into life eternally ever after.

At that point of truth, one ignites from its own ashes, and discovers a worldview that can never be taught, only felt, like a feather in the hand f the blind, a drumbeat throbbing through its own shell.

On the other side of this gripping exhale, life can only swing ahead with favor, for it has already known the painful risk of flying backwards.

I raise my heels into the air, and lean into the light, yarns of gold fanning the magical fall breeze like a dream catcher for the new rising sun.

Because He loves me, He will catch me. God will stop my world. I feel His hands on my back, and lay my faith solely in Him. Impossibility is only the offspring of man.

EIGHT

Nightshade

This cocoon is cozy and cold, the only heat roasting from our hearts, flowing through the comfort of furry coats and a cape of cashmere. Despite the wisdom of the day, we are not without but incandescently *within*, our innocence singing again, feet afloat by oak coals and flinted embers.

How revealing life becomes apart from the world—our selves never the same, for we emerged from the debris with minds silenced, natural and blessed with the solitude of castaways, our voices together a ringing soliloquy in the forest of destruction.

At night, we turn on the moon, its light flashing down on the primitive sign chilled into the sand, a prayer of mercy sketched into a rough heart, the Indian summer setting on our long list of farewells.

Here at our place, we have been awakened like paper whites blooming through the frost of life, alive in God's chrysalis before becoming buckeyes born of the fortune of His light.

Free and in love with every frigid green space, my deco wings touch peace in the steel ruffles of thyme as winter creeps, the coquette mums on their last eight o'clock of the season, raspberries fall into gold on the vine.

Morning arrives as our only timepiece, before the moist tropical river mist clings to our soiled coveralls, stained with fruitful work, despite the drooping chains of nightshade that lure us into despondency by rest.

In this wildest existence, grace comes to each evening meal, and again, day dawns to His spirit sewing us into new skins, shedding self-love for denim legs and canvassed hands, and at breaking hour, the smoky, intoxicating breath of the sweetest cider overflows our dry cups with its seductive hazy curls suspended like clouds amidst the greyest of suns.

I am ripe for a coming, all the while waiting, hoeing and praying for the advent of compassion, knowing He comes like tomorrow's dew, and morning always has its own cast.

NINE

Missing *in Lafayette*

Presently, I am the absent mother as a performance takes place, one I would never dare imagine missing, much less slumbering through. The irresponsible alarm rings late, screeching imperfection, intolerant of an honest mistake.

The cleansing of an herbal bath is far from relieving, powerless to drown the screams of guilt I hear beneath the steaming water. The tonic of humility cannot excuse the unspeakable, and I strive to create words that measure regret in adequate doses. The perfect never-wills, high values, impenetrable standards I have brought with me into this new life must depart, for I can no longer hold their demanding attention.

Months ago, a crisis would have been declared, but now alone, a calmer, smaller self is emerging from the towering ego of pain. The shame will not overtake my center of all-knowing peace, and a silver seam beams through the foggy morning as His consolations cheer my soul.

Instead of blame, I write, finding I remain the good mother, albeit the porcelain service has been broken and swept into a pile of unfortunate circumstances, and my anchor of approval still drops in the rising water.

He reminds me that I have been rich in good works, raised children, shown hospitality, washed many feet and been devoted to family, yet despite all reassurance, this omission keeps me lacking like a needle begging for thread. Single again, an imaginary widow spinning an empty web with bare spools, still questioning men and mothers, "Are you my God?"

What if I am not a lady of proverb, what if I stumble and fall, see and own the land but make no sense of it all; knowing no man or husband, except for the divine. Yet all I have ever known is what's mine is mine alone. Will the world love me the same? And does anyone care?

Good and evil, I am a creature of a different sort now, a servant of love, answering only to my husband above, who uses the dew of tears for good, to glisten my silken tent, including the holes I sew alone.

TEN

Jasper *at Mount Magazine*

There are moments in the wilderness when the trees have no order, when one stumbles along the forest floor and only the mountain peaks. Life is silent and finally God is allowed to speak.

These conversations are the most captivating, an awakening of the soul eminent, yet confounded when asked how one survives in the thicket of uncertainty, when only the thinnest of air sighs clarity. Up the stained copper paths, the monastic way seems even more undefined and mysterious. Only He owns my whereabouts, and I am hopelessly lost in maples sugared and jasper scattered, clay bluffs rolling seamlessly for miles yonder along Route 22.

CHAPTER TEN

The deepest of topaz has been carved around my footprints, and it seems well fitting that this lonely visitor has disappeared into divine presence, my silhouette treading through the puzzle of unheard echoes, wishing for the rivers of home seducing me with security.

Instead it is dry as I gaze below the wild sky into the purpled herringbone vale and understand why God dangles us above this opening dusty vault—to bring us closer, higher to ourselves—to lose all belongings to these foothills of heaven.

For who we are is nothing yet precious, a tiniest sparkle in mines of seas, a fleck of flint in deserts of lands, a nugget buried in the tombs of earth. In this smallness we find Him finding our beauty, infilling, one breath after another, purpose into confusion, steadiness into struggle, hope into tender despair.

He detects our small, fragile souls and meets us under the immensity of vespers, alone where our identities are outshone, invisible and overpowered by perfect love.

It is His gold, His gift and my bronze could never dare compare.

ELEVEN

Lucky

Our song is rain and the bewitching night is young. It is always by his way, his calling, my obedient feelings emerge from their bedchamber, a syllable from his voice sufficient to rouse their startling in the chartreuse leaves.

I am settled in when the truth is made to my talisman that he has been a matter of inspiration, a writer's muse, our secrets kept on tablets even after our eyes blinked goodbye. Now he wants to make mystery.

Long ago, I believed he was a god mate, later, a lucky gift. But now I am certain this kind of love is best left untouched in its crystal cave, away from the rush of watershed, safe from pools of needs; a promise honored more by friendship than cascading into far more than destined to be.

Yet, desire often undresses reason, and as the thunder claps with God's displeasure, I am disobediently locked in love like a reckless carriage that keeps driving back to its temptress, his charming will smothering my thoughts, until my veil of wisdom is torn with a brooch of delight.

Does God shutter his knowing eyes and turn off the light, momentarily giving up on our foolish acts like the fit of a mother with a stubborn child burning with fever? When we fail does He go into a room of his own or carry us home?

Can He hear our silent sorry and is guilt bigger than His forgiveness?

Mercy creaks the stained floor, and I feel the tendrils of breath moving closer until my head is at one with His kiss, reassured there is never a moment, a sigh of surrender, a pause, in which my torment suspends His love.

One has the choice, at every detour on the journey, to share the spirit or lose honor; wish good tidings or harm the lens of the soul; let love flash away or live in the desire of woman; or simply find a friend for such a time as this.

This game I vow to end tonight, counting passion a price I could never afford, casting my lot and bartering the fable for peace, knowing we are best as minstrels of the path, a misstep of this broken fall.

TWELVE

Carousel

The days spin, chaos circles and catches my will to be on a peaceful plane, content in all circumstances, not just desired pleasures, but the disruptive experiences that keep us moving without progress, growing without visible markings, the ups and downs of enlightenment without any real measurements of forward motion.

The ego gets lost, blurred on this unfamiliar ride that the soul seems called to, the joyful, weightless carousel that make all things familiar very vague, almost absent, especially the images of people and things once special and important, the influences once pleasurable, now left behind as one embarks on a new course and follows a different light.

This opportunity usually appears in the wilderness, where profound conversions often find their time, meet their destiny and forever change one's relationship to the past world.

It occurs when one's soul finally recognizes its value, accepts and believes its power over self-concern and ego domination. What once was, no longer is. What is feels uncertain but true, real and persuasive.

The "Who am I?" is answered by I AM.

And on that day, or year, an internal clash occurs with everything modern culture promotes and values—independence, monetary gain, ambition, and the false security of a magical ending, the end reward of daily personal sacrifice.

Yet somehow the harder one works, looks and seeks, the farther the line recedes until that empty circle of life becomes a zero—a disaster, reversal of fortune, divorce, or in my case, all of the above.

Maddening, disappointing, incredibly frightening, yet all divine opportunities for a remarkable spiritual encounter.

In all of my despair, rationalizing and suffering, the same cataclysmic events shook all of the heavens to unlock the mystical miracle of grace. I have learned here, in the wilds, how restoration can supercede the pain of loss, how in the darkness, one's soul is only a prayer away, a night away from a great spiritual awakening. Only alone do we discover that we are not alone.

My God is waiting, right now, if only I recognize his encouragement, believe His promise, trust in His plan, even when I no longer recognize my own existence.

I have lost everything, but gained more than one can absorb with small eyes. My heart has been broken, yet it now holds more than its tiny capacity ever could. I have begged to die and know now, that I already have.

And that is precisely where He wants me, needs me, so He can love me, mold me, find me, and use me.

THIRTEEN

Sunshine

There are some men who rely upon the strength of their own hands, ingenuity and true craft to make their way in life, speaking the accent of kindness more intently than configuring their words in order to prove themselves, for their only asylum has always been themselves, as though God has imparted His own soul into theirs without their knowledge, or consent. Men of the risen South are that humble and unassuming to assume otherwise.

In the wooded fields, their ambition sows without demanding any sort of harvest, for it is simply respectful and responsible to the land entrusted to its labor.

They live and work for a legacy, generations more but never for the gratification of today, for detachment is their best protection against pride. To collect luxuries would be to forfeit the spirit of freedom, and while they understand all the subtleties of nature, for instance, the preferences of a doe, the chase of a young buck; the sun's rotation on plant life; the habits of carpenter bees; and their like; any intellectual pursuit or self-serving gain would alone sacrifice all they have ever known—self-belief.

Trusting in instincts and natural intelligence protects all frivolity from stretching their pockets in directions they cannot afford, thus their only balance is by accounting for their work at day's end, often into the small horizon of nightfall, when the dusk settles the stirrings of the day, quiets the songbirds and moans for rain.

At this time, they retire to an uncommon satisfaction, an abiding peace found when the boots rest on the porch and the wages are aright for the hours. Nothing is owed for tomorrow, yesterday settled in full with a handful of dollars and a basket of fresh catch.

Along this countryside, I am encountering these men of overlooked virtues, one particularly kind-hearted, and his deserving wife, who has elected to manage my stockpiles of torn trees, un-mended fences and strewn tin roofs.

Each day, his sunshine clears the long shell drive, yet rarely do we speak anything substantial, for it is far more satisfactory to acknowledge without intervening or interrupting another's area. That would begin an arrangement less fortunate, for business here hardly involves pleasantries or hell-ows, just an eyeful of respect before getting on with the strapping of nails or searing of the saw.

I perform neither, watching only through broken windows, imagining how civilization began in a world much the same, yet drastically far from its roots.

Sometimes, I find sticks without any under-standing of how to make them nestle into a flame, or a bird I admire, but have hardly observed much life to identify with name.

How foolish the city makes our existence—infantile, burdensome—when there is a brave calling and too few hunting its sound.

Instead, ignorance is stoked in rocked fireplaces, dinner frozen on pewter, bicycles bolted into a high-rise, life endured without any means to pay the fair price for the privilege. Reckoning in the darkness, all accounting is far away and night unbearable for the lost modernfolk.

Their masters will arrive in the morning on subways before the fast breaks and leave last to protect the steel-walled insanity. I myself now stare at the rubble and wonder how He ever found me there.

Tubular *in New York*

There is so much pain in this world, and I have forgotten, after images that still flood and haunt my
dreams, how hard it is to find the good when man is
in control of our remote fears. I have been shielding
myself from this reality since losing all power,
the disseminator of negative news indefinitely
unplugged.

Restoring its waves of digital doom has been a
lost priority, and its lost luster lingers with regret at
every switch.

I have hardly missed the hiss, content to spend
the now sparse hours of inactivity reading, thinking,
or just noticing how the changing leaves are a shade
deeper than seasons past.

But last night, my last night here in an alive alluring East Coast city, I turned on its company, an artificial accessory I have not heard in these months without communications.

It amazes me how one never misses what it hated hearing, the grim and the heartbreak that seem to replicate the tragedies I pray never to witness or endure again.

Suffering still stalwarts all joy, visually reducing my soul to the shame of nothing prime—only primal—relaying the realization that this plastic bubble I balance may be worn as its wand, but not completely dissolved like so many images in its dim rainbow glaze.

Is this the world God created or is our sight distorted?

Comparing misery, mine seems surprisingly brighter, which makes one wonder if I should darken the screen tonight, will all look better in the morning? And can the blessing multiply across the airwaves long enough so that all the world will see only one dark hole in homes, and hopefully realize its equally blackening effect on billions of chances for peace.

Would our world stop to change or follow yet another messenger? Do we beg for its poor pain or is true reality changing channels, tuning out, indifferently ignoring its false energy?

As the lights streak the shades, and sirens color the white noise, these questions bring my heart where often the mind denies going, to the only connection permanent, impenetrable and to all things, good.

FIFTEEN

Christes Maesse

In the deep white footprints of December, the angel's hair feathers the silvery laurels, and all of heaven's tears seep down the millions of boughs of peace.

It must befool Him to be so far from the embrace of Calvary—strung on storefronts and hung on trees, to hear His unsung lessons lost amongst the masses of idols, misguiding the Trinity star to descend behind our colored stones of nothingness.

How we diminish all meaning of His season— the Holy Family, the purity and reverence of His spiritual gifts when we use the nails to hang our own decorations and desires.

In all of our pagan hustling and feasting, it seems only Bethlehem is awake in glory, for here, there are far too many people to ever notice Him coming, far too many places and scenes to ever find our knees.

When did merry friends, colleagues and even family don our crown, come as king, brighten the desolate desert with universal love, walk as a man-child sifting the dust of sinners?

Who are we worshipping tonight?

Christes Maesse is a life-saving blessing, an ideal one must hold with all trust, like the babe in the woods, never allowing strangers near, for nurturing and protecting its honor, in turn, has an equal effect on mankind. Our King is and always should remain untouchable, invincible and celebrated.

So, on that joyous morning of his coming, we rejoiced in sequins and tiaras, adorning the table with beautiful flowers and over-the-top fancies. Christmas is an idea and ideal that few may truly understand; but as for myself, I shall never worship a jolly man or merry time. For my soul shall glorify the Lord.

He alone is sufficient and holy, we undeserving, collectively unconscious of the magnificence.

For when we find our love in the manger, we truly begin to love the world. When we see our King in the sky, we begin to watch our way. When we know our promise born, only then do we possess trust.

What was promised was delivered far above what all dare ask or imagine. Yet, of all the presents I stare for the stones and the nails, and wonder: Where is Immanuel? And who stole His honor?

SIXTEEN

Darkhouse *on the First*

Every New Year's Eve in New Orleans the fog sets into a seasonally heavy ground cloud, and this year is no exception, albeit a most exceptional year in my history.

The weighty, eerie illusion of it all kept close travelers distant, despite futile attempts to caravan and control the dark, dense despair, of which only patches of glimmering dark houses sparingly revealed roads and paths, out, never into, the remains of a city exiled and ended, not in glory, only with horror.

I have never been more absorbed into a storm of haunted moisture, nor blinded by faith where indeed, my soul mate could be resurrected out of the rubble.

For days, with only faith as fiction, I attempted to complete my mission—to fulfill divine instruction when every symptom in the natural manifests into madness, like lunacy on a moonless night, when sanity sinks lower than melted mausoleums mourn.

I persevere and bridge the soupy span, thickened by midnight, a snaked stretch of bridge locals loaded on that frightful day prior to September past to find salvation.

Not mine, of course, for that occurred forever and many a miracle ago. But when your soul is so intertwined with another's, and every clinging street sign clouded by judgment, His will begins to look like ours—not just mine anymore.

If angels really do exist in America, it is completely certain their spirits are hovering hard and fast over the lost in lockdown here, beckoning believers like myself, whose personal philosophies elegantly escaped relevance and relocated to higher ground, to join their crusade.

The man God has chosen for me is in every way the most unholy of choices most days, yet pure and wounded honestly to a fault. And that precise fault line is as jaggedly jaded as my positioning on this road to redemption.

For hours I comb airless alleys and suffocated streets, smoked with death, remains of fire powder and loud crackers crumbled, visible only upon the descent by the sheer scrim of headlights.

It is terrifying and fatally fatalistic, for my security is still celebrating on the side remaining, where hands of time are struck back and still, surreal and staid, not like this place I try and cry for.

A queen ship aground, unconscious and defenseless, dumped on the dry dock of death.

A new year has been born again, and yet my plan, swelled and swollen in the evaporated rains, lay breathless and lifeless with winds of wreckage.

Until God arrived and rocketed the revelry.

I now find myself on foot in the weaning hours of an infant year, meandering quarters of bungalows where the enemy edifies this contagious city one sin at a time. Historic high rises and folksy funhouses disappear within one block's wrong turn, absent only His footprints forever flushed by the war of nature.

How does one's soul stumble here? A misstep? Misuse and abuse? Misery?

I kept questioning and searching before finding the fallen one lost amongst the wanderlust and wonder, darkly luminous, too close to the other side for comfort.

Even later, as he slept away, and I drove away, across the shore the lighthouse kept watching the waters, flickering, resting soundly with grace.

www.ingramcontent.com/pod-product-compliance
Lightning Source LLC
Chambersburg PA
CBHW030657270326
41929CB00007B/403